Soccer: Attacking

Barbara Bonney

The Rourke Press, Inc.
Vero Beach, Florida 32964

PHOTO CREDITS
All photos © Glen Benson

ACKNOWLEDGMENTS
The author wishes to acknowledge Doug Semark for his contribution in writing this book

EDITORIAL SERVICES:
Penworthy Learning Systems

Library of Congress Cataloging-in-Publication Data

Bonney, Barbara, 1955-
  Soccer: Attacking / Barbara Bonney.
    p. cm. — (Soccer)
  Includes index.
  Summary: Presents various kinds of soccer attacks, such as dribbling, passing, and several different kicking techniques.
   ISBN 1-57103-135-9
   1. Soccer—Offense—Juvenile literature. [1. Soccer.]
I. Title II. Series: Bonney, Barbara, 1955- Soccer.
GV943.9.044B65 1997
796.334'23—DC21   97-8096
                                                     CIP
                                                     AC

Printed in the USA

TABLE OF CONTENTS

THE PURPOSE OF ATTACKING

In soccer, when a team has the ball, they are **attacking** (uh TACK ing). The purpose of attacking is to keep control of the ball, to move the ball toward the goal, and to get the ball into the goal. If the other team gets the ball, that team becomes the attackers. A team keeps control of the ball by moving it and protecting it from the **defenders** (di FEND erz).

Dribbling is an important part of attacking.

The attackers move the ball and protect it from defenders.

DRIBBLING

When a player is running and moving the ball with feet, it is called **dribbling** (DRIB ling). Using the instep of the foot, where the shoe laces are, the ball is gently kicked just ahead of the runner, who kicks it gently again when he/she catches up to it. The kicks should land just under

Keeping the ball is hard work when defenders stay close.

Dribbling is safest when no defenders are near.

the center of the ball. The safest place to dribble is on the sides, or wings, of the field. Dribbling is always risky when a defender is close enough to take the ball. Dribbling is used to get away from a defending player or when you cannot pass to a teammate.

PASSING

Passing, or giving the ball to a teammate, is important in attacking. Passing and dribbling both move the ball toward to the goal. Dribbling is used when the ball is not in danger of being stolen by defenders. Passing is a quick way around defenders and a good way to make the ball hard to defend.

When the ball is in danger of being stolen, passing is a good move.

PREPARING TO SHOOT

If a ball is dribbled down the wings of a field, the player must find a way to get the ball in front of the goal to shoot. When the ball is moved across instead of up or down the field, the move is called crossing. Crossing halfway, or kicking the ball from the wings into the goal area, is called centering. To center, a player should aim at the farthest goal post. Either the ball will go into the goal, or it will be set up for another player to shoot it in.

Dribbling down the sides of the field leaves only one side to protect.

Centering brings the ball from the wings to the center of the field.

THROW-INS

When the ball goes past one of the **touchlines** (TUCH lynz) on the side of the field, it is out of play and the game must be restarted with a thrown-in. The assistant referee will wave the flag and give the ball to the closest player on the team that did not touch the ball last.

A throw-in begins behind the head.

A throw-in continues over the head and is then released.

The player stands near where the ball left the field and puts both feet on or behind the line. Both hands must be used to throw the ball from behind the head in an overhand style. Once the ball is thrown, the thrower cannot touch the ball again until somebody else touches it.

GOAL KICKS

When the ball last touched by an attacker, goes over the goal line, but not in the goal, the defenders are awarded a kick from the goal area. The kicker must kick the ball out of the **penalty area** (PEN ul tee AIR ee uh) without any other players touching it. Once it reaches the field it is in play.

Attacking positions can shift and overlap in soccer.

This goalkeeper was awarded a goal kick.

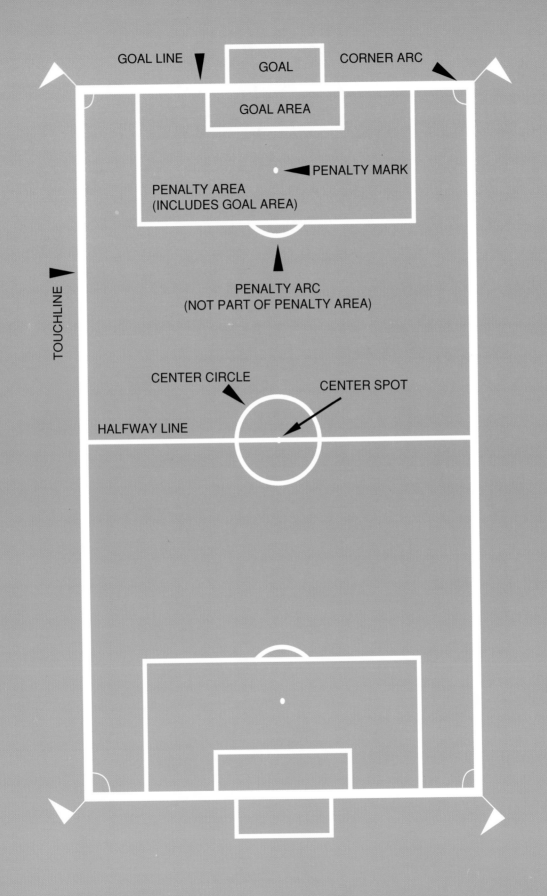

CORNER KICKS

A corner kick is much like a goal kick. The difference is in who touched the ball last. If an attacker touched it, then a goal kick is given. If a defender touched it, then a corner kick is awarded. The ball is put in the corner (where the flags are) nearest to where the ball went over the goal line. The ball must be inside the lines. Defenders must stand at least ten yards (nine meters) away until the ball is in play.

Corner kicks are played from the wedge-shaped corner areas.

17

FREE KICKS

A free kick is the reward for being **fouled** (FOWLD). A referee blows a whistle and the ball is put on the ground where the foul happened. The kick is free because the other team must stand back at least ten yards. A free kick may be direct or indirect.

A direct free kick can be shot right into the goal.

An indirect free kick must be played by someone besides the kicker before a goal can count.

A direct kick can send the ball right into the goal. It is given after a serious foul. An indirect kick has to be touched by a player before it counts as a goal. It is given for a less serious foul.

PENALTY KICKS

A penalty kick is also given for being fouled, if the foul happens in the penalty area. It is a direct free kick from inside the penalty area. All players must be outside the penalty area except the kicker and goalkeeper. Penalty kicks are rarely used in kids' soccer.

Attackers who do not have the ball should move to open areas for passes.

A penalty kick is difficult to defend.

GLOSSARY

attacking (uh TACK ing) — offensive plays; moving to get the ball into the goal

defenders (di FEND erz) — the players who defend, or guard the ball from going into the attacker's goal

dribbling (DRIB ling) — to move a ball by repeated light kicking

fouled (FOWLD) — having a rule broken against you accidentally

penalty area (PEN ul tee AIR ee uh) — the goal and the large area in front of it

touchlines (TUCH lynz) — the lines marking the sides of the soccer field

Teammates support each other by being available.

INDEX